W9-BCX-903

DATE DUE

Super Senses

Hearing

Mary Mackill

Heinemann Library
Chicago, Illinois

© 2006 Heinemann Library
a division of Reed Elsevier Inc.
Chicago, Illinois

Customer Service 888-454-2279

Visit our website at www.heinemannraintree.com

Printed and bound in China by South China Printing Company Limited
Photo research by Hannah Taylor and Fiona Orbell
Designed by Jo Hinton-Malivoire and bigtop

10 09 08 07 06
10 9 8 7 6 5 4 3 2 1

Library of Congress Cataloging-in-Publication Data
Mackill, Mary.
    Hearing / Mary Mackill.
        p. cm. -- (Super senses)
    Includes bibliographical references and index.
    ISBN 1-4034-7375-7 (library binding-hardcover) -- ISBN 1-4034-7382-X (pbk.)
  1. Taste--Juvenile literature. I. Title. II. Series: Mackill, Mary. Super senses.
QP462.2.M33 2006
612.8'5--dc22
                                                    2005018905

Acknowledgments
The publishers would like to thank the following for permission to reproduce photographs:
Alamy Images pp. **15**, **23a** (Inmagine), **7**, **23c** (Luca DiCecco); Corbis pp. **11l**, **22** (royalty free), **16** (Eye Ubiquitous; Robert & Linda Mostyn), **14**, **23b** (O'Brien Productions), **13** (Simon Marcus), **6** (Tom & Dee Ann McCarthy); Getty Images pp. **9** (Digital Vision), **4**, **11r**, **18** (Photodisc), **12** (Photographer's Choice), **17**, **19** (Stone); Harcourt Education Ltd pp. **5**, **10**, **20**, **21** (Tudor photography).

Cover photograph reproduced with permission of Harcourt Education Ltd.

Every effort has been made to contact copyright holders of any material reproduced in this book. Any omissions will be rectified in subsequent printings if notice is given to the publisher.

Many thanks to the teachers, library media specialists, reading instructors, and educational consultants who have helped develop the Read and Learn/Lee y aprende brand.

Disclaimer
All the Internet addresses (URLs) given in this book were valid at the time of going to press. However, due to the dynamic nature of the Internet, some addresses may have changed, or sites may have changed or ceased to exist since publication. While the author and publishers regret any inconvenience this may cause readers, no responsibility for any such changes can be accepted by either the author or the publishers.

The paper used to print this book comes from sustainable resources.

Contents

Some words are shown in bold, **like this**. You can find out what they mean by looking in the glossary.

What Are My Senses?

You have five **senses**. They help you see, hear, taste, smell, and touch things.

Pretend you are playing in a band.

What can you hear?

Hearing is one of our five senses.

What Do I Use to Hear?

You use your ears to hear.

Sound comes into your ears.

Your ears stick out from your head.

This helps them pick up sounds all around you.

How Do I Hear?

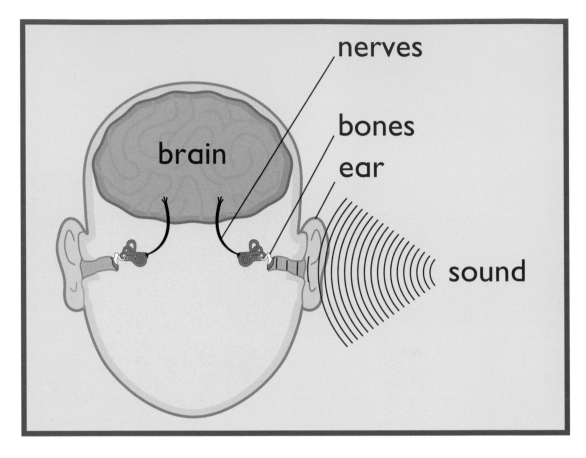

Sound hits some small **bones** in your ear.

Nerves send a message to your brain.

Your brain picks up the message.

Your brain would tell you that
these children are laughing.

What Can I Hear?

You can hear loud and quiet sounds.

truck

birds

You can hear low and high sounds.

Which makes a high sound?

How Does Hearing Help Me?

Your **sense** of hearing helps you stay safe.

You can hear cars or trains and get out of their way.

If you get lost, you can hear
someone calling you.

How Can I Hear Things Better?

A **microphone** can make people sound louder.

Headphones help you hear music better.

They keep you from hearing other sounds around you.

How Can I Take Care of My Hearing?

Loud sounds can hurt your ears.

Cover your ears to protect them.

Try to keep your ears clean.

If your ears hurt, ask your doctor
to look at them.

Animals Can Hear, Too!

Some animals can hear very well.

They can hear when danger
is near.

Some animals can hear sounds that we cannot hear.

A dog can hear very high sounds.

Test Your Sense of Hearing

Cover your friend's eyes.

Stand to one side and clap your hands.

Can your friend point to you?

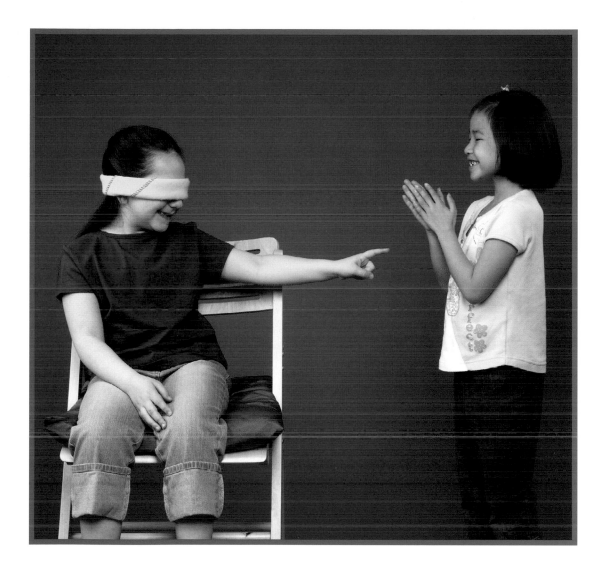

You have two ears, one on each side of your head.

This means you can hear sounds from all around you.

Hearing Is Super!

Your **sense** of hearing:

- tells you how loud or quiet something is

- warns you if something is coming toward you

- means you can listen to your friends!

Glossary

 **bone** hard part inside your body. The bones in your ear are small but very important for hearing.

 **headphones** something that covers your ears so that you can listen to music

 **microphone** something you speak into that makes the sound louder

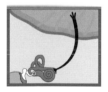 **nerve** part inside your body. Nerves work with the brain to sense things.

 **sense** something that helps you see, touch, taste, smell, and hear things around you

Index

Note to Parents and Teachers

Reading for information is an important part of a child's literacy development. Learning begins with a question about something. Help children think of themselves as investigators and researchers by encouraging their questions about the world around them. Each chapter in this book begins with a question. Read the question together. Look at the pictures. Talk about what you think the answer might be. Then read the text to find out if your predictions were correct. Think of other questions you could ask about the topic, and discuss where you might find the answers. Assist children in using the picture glossary and the index to practice new vocabulary and research skills.